Presented to

_____

On the occasion of

_____

From

_____

Date

_____

Published by Barbour Publishing, Inc., P. O. Box 719, Uhrichsville, Ohio 44683 http://www.barbourbooks.com

Member of the
Evangelical Christian
Publishers Association

Printed in China.

HEAVEN

GLIMPSES OF GLORY

Written and Compiled by
Ellyn Sanna

BARBOUR
PUBLISHING, INC.

Heaven is the presence of God.
CHRISTINA ROSSETTI

*I*f this world we live in now, the world we can see and hear and touch, is the only reality, then death casts its long dark shadow over even the loveliest moments, for one day all of this life's sweetness will come to an end. But if there is something more beyond this world, then the meaning of death changes altogether. Instead of being life's dark end, death becomes the doorway into a fuller, brighter reality.

God's Word tells us that heaven *is* a fact. It's not just a pretty fairy tale human beings have told each other down through the centuries to comfort themselves against death's creeping darkness. Heaven is the kingdom of God that will last forever. It is a brilliant, solid reality that will make our lives here look like mere shadows. And through Christ's redemption, it is our true home where we will live joyfully, now and through all eternity.

Then shall the King say. . . ,
"Come, ye blessed of my Father,
inherit the kingdom prepared for you
from the foundation of the world."
MATTHEW 25:34

1

THE KINGDOM OF GOD

The kingdom of heaven is like to a grain of mustard seed,
which a man took, and sowed in his field:
Which indeed is the least of all seeds:
but when it is grown, it is the greatest among herbs,
and becometh a tree,
so that the birds of the air come and lodge in the branches thereof.
MATTHEW 13:31–32

More than anything else, heaven is the kingdom of God, the place where God's will is acted out in concrete reality. When we think of heaven in these terms, then we realize that it is not only some far-off, golden city; it is also here on earth. It grows in our lives from the tiniest of seeds, and its life spreads and deepens, intersecting our earthly reality. Through Christ, we are already inhabitants of His kingdom.

A Place of Abundance and Restoration

*T*he smallest grain of seed becomes a tree that birds can nest in. The emphasis is purely on heaven's magnitude. For in moving from thoughts of earth to thoughts of heaven, we have to visualize an expansion of the kind that converts a seed into a tree. And, of course, our Lord gave concrete expression to this aspect of heaven as a place of abundance beyond earthly dreams when he took the five loaves and the two small fishes and transformed them into a meal for five thousand people.

The gravest earthly deprivation which life in heaven will correct is the loss of our loved ones. For the Christian the past which is irrecoverable on earth is recoverable in heaven.

Harry Blamires,
Knowing the Truth about Heaven and Hell

When the eyes of the soul looking out
meet the eyes of God looking in,
heaven has begun right here on this earth.
A. W. TOZER,
The Pursuit of God

The kingdom of heaven is not
come even when God's will is our law;
it is fully come when God's will is our will.
GEORGE MACDONALD

As our knowledge and our love of God increase,
by the same degree and in the same proportion
the kingdom of an inward heaven
must necessarily increase also.
JOHN WESLEY

hrough hope we already dwell in heaven. . . . The one thing necessary is to believe, and to pray with complete confidence in the name of Christ. . . . Without our help, counsel, thought, or effort, He Himself alone has brought forth His Kingdom, advanced it and preserved it to this day. I have not the slightest doubt that He will consummate it without our advice or assistance.

MARTIN LUTHER

*I wanted no other heaven than Jesus,
who shall be my joy when I come there.*
JULIAN OF NORWICH

Whosoever will reign with Christ in heaven
must have Christ reigning in him on earth.
JOHN WESLEY

Wherever God dwells there is heaven.
TERESA OF AVILA

Earth's crammed with heaven,
And every common bush afire with God.
ELIZABETH BARRETT BROWNING

∞

Lord, may I dwell in Your kingdom today and forever.

2

ETERNAL LIFE

But whosoever drinketh of the water that
I shall give him shall never thirst;
but the water that I shall give him shall be
in him a well of water springing up into everlasting life.
JOHN 4:14

We are so bound by the conventions of earthly thinking that it is hard for us to grasp heaven and eternity. Our thoughts are shaped by commercials and TV shows, the scientific method and Western philosophy; and through it all, we cling desperately to this life, hiding our heads like ostriches from death's dark reality.

We may call ourselves followers of Christ, but we have lost sight of what the Gospel really means. This is the Good News that Jesus brought to earth: Through Him, we will be healed and made whole—and we will live forever.

Your life has come down from heaven. . .
and took away our death,
calling us to return to Him in heaven.
Will you not now at last rise with Him and live?
AUGUSTINE

I wonder if our eagerness to hold on to this life does not
suggest that we have lost contact with one of the most
essential aspects of our creed: the faith in eternal life.
HENRI J. M. NOUWEN

The true home of a Christian is
in the heavenly realm with Christ
and in a body of immortality and glory.
PETER TOON

SAVED FOR ETERNITY

I grew up in a church that used the word *saved* a lot. It was one of those terms we said and heard so often that we no longer stopped to think what the word really meant. And then one day, death crept up close to me, and I began to wonder if this well-used word meant anything at all.

Webster says that *to save* means "to rescue or deliver from danger or harm," or "to preserve or guard from injury, destruction, or loss." As a child, I used to picture Christ rescuing me from some terrible danger—throwing me a lifesaver when I was drowning, carrying me in His arms from a burning house—and then I'd picture Him keeping me, treasuring me, the same way I liked to "save" all sorts of things on the shelves of my bedroom.

So now, having faced grief and loss, I wondered if Christ really could "save" me. It wasn't hell I feared, but nothingness. I could not bear to think that one day I might simply cease to be. The fear that the same would happen to the people I loved was a constant nightmare lurking at the edges of my thoughts.

But like a lifesaver being tossed into dark, stormy water, like strong arms carrying me through black smoke, in the midst of my pain and turmoil that worn word I had taken for granted for years began to gleam. I understood anew that Christ redeems my life from destruction (Psalm 103:4). Through Christ, we will never be thrown away; instead, we will be "preserved blameless unto the coming of our Lord Jesus Christ" (1 Thessalonians 5:23). We are truly saved.

For God so loved the world, that he gave his only begotten Son,
that whosoever believeth in him should not perish,
but have everlasting life.
JOHN 3:16

hank You, Lord,
for the gift of eternal life through Jesus.

3

GOOD-BYE TO THE SHADOW-LANDS

These are they which came out of great tribulation,
and have washed their robes,
and made them white in the blood of the Lamb.
REVELATION 7:14

In this life, all of us, sooner or later, face difficulty and hardship, pain and sorrow. We try to hold on to the people and places we love most, but eventually time or death takes them from us. No matter how tight we clutch them to our hearts, they slip away like shadows.

From our earthly perspective, the comfort heaven offers our aching hearts seems insubstantial and hazy. But when we get there, we may find that our lives here were the insubstantial shadows—while heavenly reality is more solid, more concrete, more *real* than anything we had ever imagined.

Though what if earth
Be but a shadow of heaven?
JOHN MILTON

But what, you ask, of earth?
Earth, I think, will not be found by
anyone to be in the end a very distinct place.
I think earth, if chosen instead of heaven,
will turn out to have been, all along,
only a region in hell:
and earth, if put second to heaven,
to have been from the beginning
a part of heaven itself.
C. S. LEWIS,
The Great Divorce

We are so used to thinking of death as terrifying and dark. But perhaps in reality it will be like waking up from a bad dream—or like springing out of bed on the first day of a summer vacation. . . .

All of you are—
as you used to call it in the Shadow-Lands—dead.
The term is over: the holidays have begun.
The dream is ended: this is the morning.
C. S. LEWIS,
The Last Battle

Heaven at present is out of sight,
but in due time, as snow melts and
discovers what it lay upon,
so will this visible creation fade away
before those greater splendors which are behind it.
JOHN HENRY NEWMAN

The vision that the saved in heaven will have of the love
of Christ will go far beyond even our greatest insight here,
as far as the sun's light at noon goes beyond
the light of a flickering candle at midnight.
JOHN BUNYAN

But that was not the real Narnia.
That had a beginning and an end.
It was only a shadow or a copy of the real Narnia,
which has always been here and always will be here:
just as our own world, England and all,
is only a shadow or copy of something in Aslan's real world.
. . .All of the old Narnia that mattered,
all the dear creatures, have been drawn into the real
Narnia through the Door.
And of course it is different;
as different as a real thing is from
a shadow or as waking life is from a dream.
C. S. LEWIS,
The Last Battle

A Child's Vision of Heaven

I was four years old and the house was dark around me as I huddled under the covers of my little bed. There were *things* out there in the darkness, I was sure of it. Wasn't that something lurking over there in the dark place behind the door? And something else, big and black, was looming in the corner near the dresser. No doubt there were things hiding under my bed as well. I didn't know what kinds of things were waiting out there, and that made it much worse. I held myself very still, hardly breathing, and tried to pray to Jesus for help. He could clean all the scary things out of my room.

I was lying with my eyes wide open, afraid to shut them, when suddenly, I saw a hand. It was a wonderful hand, strong and reassuring, and it held a picture out in front of me so I could see it. The picture was of heaven; it was a beautiful city, golden and shining, and it was wonderfully comforting. I looked at the picture and knew that everything would be okay; God was looking after me, and the things of my fears that had been skulking in the shadows were driven away by the glory shining out from His radiant city.

SHEILA STEWART

*M*ost of us fear the unknown—and consequently, we can't help but fear death. But God has been with us since our conception. . .and even when we reach death's boundary, He will lead us. The shadows will all fall behind us as we cross over into the light.

*L*ord, remind me often that this world is
only a shadow of what You have in store for me.

4

HOME AT LAST

There are many rooms in my Father's home,
and I am going to prepare a place for you. . . .
When everything is ready,
I will come and get you.
JOHN 14:2–3 (NLT)

All of us have times when our hearts are full of a restless longing. Sometimes, we try to fill that aching emptiness with earthly things: a new relationship, a new house, a trip to new places. These things may distract us for a while, but in the end we are always left wanting something. . .more.

That yearning hunger in our hearts is normal and healthy, though. We were created for heaven. . .and we will be homesick until at last we live in the place Jesus has prepared for us there.

Rest comes at length; though life be long and dreary,
The day must dawn, and darksome night be past;
Faith's journey ends in welcome to the weary,
And heaven, our heart's true home, will come at last.
FREDERICK W. FABER

For the power Thou hast given me to lay hold of
things unseen:
For the strong sense I have that this is not my home:
For my restless heart which nothing finite can satisfy:
I give Thee thanks, O God.
JOHN BAILLIE

FACE TO FACE AT LAST

*T*he thought of death frightens us, but I suspect its reality will astound us and fill us with birthday-party joy. After all, in that moment, as we enter heaven, we will finally see our Savior's face.

I think maybe that experience will be a little like the moments when I first saw my children. I had loved each baby for nine long months; they had been real and living parts of my life. But when I reached out and took their solid, warm little bodies in my arms, my joy spilled over. It was like coming home—not my old childhood home, but a new home that was now part of my deepest identity.

When I finally see Christ's face in heaven, no doubt I will feel that same sense of love and wonder, recognition and homecoming. Christ's presence is our true home, our perfect home, the home that's essential to our hearts' deep being. And in heaven we will never have to leave home again.

For now we see through a glass, darkly;
but then face to face: now I know in part;
but then shall I know even as also I am known.
1 CORINTHIANS 13:12

The Door That Leads to Home

It is necessary to die, but nobody wants to; you don't want to, but you are going to, willy-nilly. A hard necessity that is, not to want something which can not be avoided. If it could be managed, we would much rather not die; we would like to become like the angels by some other means than death. "We have a building from God," says St. Paul, "a home not made with hands, everlasting in heaven. For indeed we groan, longing to be clothed over with our dwelling from heaven; provided, though we be found clothed, and not naked. For indeed we who are in this dwelling place groan, being burdened; in that we do not wish to be stripped, but to be covered over, so that what is mortal may be swallowed up by life." We want to reach the kingdom of God, but we don't want to travel by way of death. And yet there stands Necessity saying: "This way, please." Do you hesitate, man, to go this way, when this is the way that God came to you?

AUGUSTINE

PERFECTLY AT HOME

*O*ur body. . .shall be raised in power, without the tendency to get sick or weak, a glorious, spiritual body. Its brightness will be like the sky's, it will shine like the stars forever and ever, it will shine like the sun. This inferior body that we have now will become like the glorious body of Jesus Christ. . . .

Now, when body and soul are finally completely united, who can imagine the glory they will possess? At last they will achieve their full potential; they will be all that God originally created them to be, totally united, with no jarring division between them so that they can serve the Lord with shouts of thanksgiving, a crown of everlasting joy upon their head.

In this world we will never have the total harmony, the oneness of body and soul that we will have in heaven. Here the body sometimes sins against the soul, and the soul burdens and annoys the body with its fears and worries. While we are in this world, the body often hangs this way, while the soul hangs that way; the two are always pulling at each other in opposite directions. But in heaven they shall have such perfect union that they will never jolt back and forth again. . . . Both will be perfectly at home and comfortable, in a way that goes beyond this world's words and thoughts.

JOHN BUNYAN,
The Riches of Bunyan

*A characteristic of genuine pilgrims is
that their journey is dominated by thoughts
of their goal and by their intense desire to reach it.
May Christians call themselves pilgrims
if they do not actually daily long
for the heavenly realm?*
PETER TOON

*"I have come home at last!
This is my real country! I belong here.
This is the land I have been looking for
all my life, though I never knew it till now."*
C. S. LEWIS,
The Last Battle

HOMECOMING

One emotion was very strong—that of homecoming. Jesus opened his home to me and seemed to say, "Here is where you belong." The words he spoke to his disciples, "In my Father's house there are many places to live in. . . . I am going now to prepare a place for you" (John 14:2), became very real. The risen Jesus, who now dwells with his Father, was welcoming me home after a long journey.

This experience was the realization of my oldest and deepest desires. Since the first moment of consciousness, I have had the desire to be with Jesus. Now I felt his presence in a most tangible way, as if my whole life had come together and I was being enfolded in love. The homecoming had a real quality of return, a return to the womb of God. The God who had fashioned me in secret and molded me in the depths of the earth, the God who had knitted me together in my mother's womb, was calling me back after a long journey and wanted to receive me back as someone who had become child enough to be loved as a child.

HENRI J. M. NOUWEN,
Beyond the Mirror

Then the new earth and sky, the same yet not the same
as these, will rise in us as we have risen in Christ.
And once again, after who knows what eons of the silence
and the dark, the birds will sing and the waters flow, and
lights and shadows move across the hills, and the faces of
our friends laugh upon us with amazed recognition.
C. S. LEWIS,
The Joyful Christian

And so, brethren, in this life we are pilgrims;
we sigh in faith for our true country
which we are unsure about.
Why do we not know the country whose citizens we are?
Because we have wandered so far away
that we have forgotten it.
But the Lord Christ, the king of the land, came down to us,
and drove forgetfulness from our heart.
God took to Himself our flesh so that
He might be our way back.
AUGUSTINE

WELCOME HOME

*I*n June, 1952, my wife of nineteen years was taken by coronary thrombosis. . . . I left the house at 1 P.M. . . . When I returned at 5:30, she was lying on the bathroom floor. There were no good-byes. She was gone.

It was probably between 1 and 2 A.M. before I got to bed and to sleep that night. However, at very early dawn I began to be conscious again of the world around me and of another world. . . .

How can I try to describe to you my experience of that dawn? All I can say is that Margaret was there and I was there at a little distance observing it all. As a Navy officer during the war, I found myself thinking of the ceremony when an admiral is piped aboard. It was as if the boundaries between earth and heaven were obliterated and Margaret was being piped aboard. She was entering her heavenly home in a blaze of glory with the birds singing that morning as I have never heard them sing before or since. It was as if ten thousand angels were crying "Joy! Joy! Here comes Margaret! Everybody out! Everybody out! Here comes Margaret!"

in *To Live Again*
by CATHERINE MARSHALL

O Christ, do thou my soul prepare
For that bright home of love
That I may see thee and adore,
With all thy saints above.
FREDERICK W. FABER

Let us come home at last to you O Lord,
so that we shall not be lost. . .
for our home is your eternity.
AUGUSTINE

Let me never forget, Lord,
that my real home is in heaven.

5

HAPPILY EVER AFTER

God shall wipe away all tears from their eyes.
REVELATION 7:17

*To rest in God eternally is the supreme joy of Heaven.
Indeed, Heaven has no meaning but that.*
BEDE JARRETT

All good stories end with "and they lived happily ever after." This
is not merely a fairy-tale ending. The best story, the truest story—
the Gospel's story—ends the same way.

To die is different from what any one supposed.
WALT WHITMAN

Heaven is where God dwells and where dwell other beings,
whether of human stock or not, who enjoy eternal bliss.
The Lord's prayer wastes no words.
It is concise and economical.
But it contains a second clear reference to heaven.
"Thy will be done, in earth as it is in heaven."
Heaven is where everything is as it should be.
HARRY BLAMIRES

IN HEAVEN, WE WILL NEVER BE BORED OR TIRED AGAIN. . .

*R*esting and vacationing are not merely being away from that which tires and wearies, saddens and depresses. We know from experience how exhilarating and invigorating a vacation can be. We shall enter into God's own Sabbath-rest, which is certainly not into inertia and boredom. . . . Rest is perfect and unruffled life, and this will be our inheritance as we, too, are wholly satisfied and fulfilled as we "vacation" in our contemplation of God—of what He has done, is doing and shall do for us. And we shall enter into this rest even as we also serve the Lord in ways which now we cannot imagine or know; like God Himself, we shall both rest and work simultaneously, and we shall never get bored or tired.

PETER TOON,
Longing for Heaven

Joy Is the Business of Heaven

I do *not* think that the life of Heaven bears any analogy to play or dance in respect of frivolity. I do think that while we are in this "valley of tears," cursed with labor, hemmed round with necessities, tripped up with frustrations, doomed to perpetual plannings, puzzlings, and anxieties, certain qualities that must belong to the celestial condition have no chance to get through, can project no image of themselves, except in activities which, for us here and now, are frivolous. . . . No. . .it is only in our "hours off," only in our moments of permitted festivity, that we find an analogy. Dance and game *are* frivolous, unimportant down here; for "down here" is not their natural place. Here, they are a moment's rest from the life we were placed here to live. But in this world everything is upside down. That which, if it could be prolonged here, would be a truancy, is likest that which in a better country is the End of Ends. Joy is the serious business of Heaven.

C. S. LEWIS,
The Joyful Christian

*S*ometimes my children worry about what dying will be like. When they do, one thing I've always told them is that I think it will be a little like when they went to school for the first time: When they were three or even four years old, the thought of being away from me all day was scary and strange. But when the day came when they got on that yellow bus for kindergarten, they were not only ready; they were excited and joyful. Their earlier fears were for nothing—and when God takes us home to heaven, we will find that our worries about death were also all for nothing, as we enter into joy eternal.

An eight-year-old boy who was dying of cancer was comforted by a similar dream:

A big yellow school bus pulled up to his house in the dream and the door opened. On the bus he saw Jesus, who told him of his impending death and invited him to go with Him on the bus. In his dream, he accepted Jesus' invitation. It was with great peace that he recounted this dream to his parents.

DIANE M. KOMP, M.D.,
A Window to Heaven

THE SOUL'S BIRTHDAY

At birth a child comes forth amid pain and danger, from the narrow dwelling of the mother's womb, into the broad light of day. In a similar way a person goes through the narrow gate of death. . . . And though heaven and earth under which we now live appear so wide, so vast, yet, in comparison with the heaven that shall be, it is far narrower and much smaller than is the womb in comparison with the broad expanse of the sky. That is why the death of saints is called a new birth. . . . A woman, when she is in labor, has sorrow, because her hour has come; but as soon as she has delivered the child, she forgets her anguish. . . . Likewise in death. We wrestle in anguish, yet know that hereafter we shall come forth into a wide, open space, and into eternal joy.

MARTIN LUTHER

On this view, what we know of life so far has been one long, uncomfortable preparation, one long experience of dragging around the burden of pregnancy, one long sequence of disaster-fraught rehearsals for a performance that has yet to be put on.

HARRY BLAMIRES,
Knowing the Truth about Heaven and Hell

Delight and Pleasure

he love we have for Christ, if I may so say, will keep us busy, even when we are in heaven. I don't mean busy in the sense that we will get tired and burdened and bored, the way we do here on earth when we have to work too hard. No, this busyness will be delightful and productive and obedient. We don't know exactly what we will be doing in heaven—we don't even understand exactly what *we* will be—but we can say in a general way that there will be work there that we never complete here on earth, and this work will delight and satisfy us. . . . Some may protest that the Bible says that in heaven we will rest from our labor. True, but we won't have to rest from our delights. That which we liked best to do on earth will no longer become tiring in heaven; we will no longer suffer from exhaustion and physical pain. All the things that used to burden us will be gone, and all that will be left will be delight and pleasure.

JOHN BUNYAN,
The Riches of Bunyan

We can most truly say that they all lived happily ever after. But for them it was only the beginning of the real story. All their life in this world and all their adventures in Narnia had only been the cover and the title page: now at last they were beginning Chapter One of the Great Story, which no one on earth has read: which goes on for ever: in which every chapter is better than the one before.

C. S. LEWIS,
The Last Battle

Death can hold no bitterness for the soul that loves. . . . There is no sadness in the thought of death when it opens the door to all joy. Nor can it be painful and oppressive when it is the end of all unhappiness and sorrow and the beginning of all good.

JOHN OF THE CROSS

JOHN'S DESCRIPTION OF HEAVEN
IN THE BOOK OF REVELATION:

And I saw a new heaven and a new earth: for the first heaven and the first earth were passed away; and there was no more sea. And I John saw the holy city, new Jerusalem, coming down from God out of heaven, prepared as a bride adorned for her husband. And I heard a great voice out of heaven saying, Behold, the tabernacle of God is with men, and he will dwell with them, and they shall be his people, and God himself shall be with them, and be their God. And God shall wipe away all tears from their eyes; and there shall be no more death, neither sorrow, nor crying, neither shall there be any more pain: for the former things are passed away.

REVELATION 21:1–4

TAKE JOY!

One day we will leave this earthly life.
When we do, may we hear Christ say,
*"Well done, thou good and faithful servant. . .
enter thou into the joy of thy lord."*
MATTHEW 25:21

*No heaven can come to us unless our hearts
find rest in it today. Take Heaven.
The gloom of the world is but a shadow;
behind it, yet within our reach, is joy. Take joy.*
FRA GIOVANNI, 1513

*Lord, thank You for Your joy,
both now and for eternity.*